World Mandalas

100 DESIGNS FOR COLORING AND MEDITATION

Written and illustrated by
MADONNA GAUDING

GODSFIELD

An Hachette UK Company
www.hachette.co.uk

First published in Great Britain in 2005
by Godsfield Press, a division of Octopus Publishing Group Ltd,
Carmelite House, 50 Victoria Embankment
London EC4Y 0DZ
www.octopusbooks.co.uk
www.octopusbooksusa.com

This edition published in 2017

Distributed in the US by
Hachette Book Group USA, 1290 Avenue of the Americas,
4th and 5th Floors, New York NY 10104 USA

Distributed in Canada by
Canadian Manda Group, 664 Annette St
Toronto, Ontario, Canada M6S 2C8

ISBN 978-1-84181-477-3

Printed and bound in China

1 3 5 7 9 10 8 6 4 2

Picture Acknowledgements
Bridgeman Art Library, London/New York/www.bridgeman.co.uk/Private Collection,
Archives Charmet 13;/Private Collection, Dinodia 10. Corbis UK Ltd/Geoffrey Clements
16;/Angelo Hornak 14;/Tom Nebbia 9. Getty Images/Charles Krebs 4;/Spike Walker 7.
Lonely Planet Images/Karen Trist 12. Nasa/(NASA-HQ-GRIN) 6.

Contents

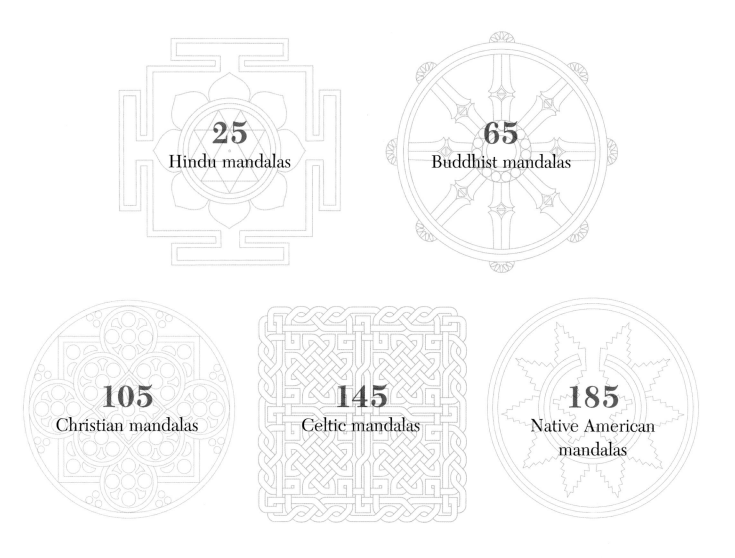

Introduction

WHAT IS A MANDALA?

A mandala is a sacred circle, a symbol of wholeness. The word *mandala* comes from the Sanskrit word meaning 'circle' or 'sacred centre'; it can also mean 'essence container'. Although the word has its origins in ancient India, this sacred symbol is found in all cultures throughout time. It is linked to sacred geometry, psychology and healing, and finds expression in art, architecture and everyday objects. Mandalas are primarily circular (although they can sometimes appear as circles or triangles within squares), and are always symmetrical and draw your eye towards the centre. As you become more aware of the mandala form, you will discover endless examples. Consider the following:

- Hildegard of Bingen, an 11th-century Benedictine abbess, painted exquisite mandala-like images depicting her mystical realizations.
- Chartres Cathedral in France has a mandala-like labyrinth designed into the floor, large enough for medieval pilgrims to trace by walking along it to the centre.
- The Pantheon in Rome, Italy, a perfectly round building built in 25 BCE, was originally designed to house a circle of images of Roman gods and goddesses.
- Tibetan Buddhist mandalas are symbolic representations of the sacred home of Buddhist deities.

A kaleidoscope creates a mandala with pink dahlias.

- Native American sand paintings featuring mandala patterns are used in traditional healing rituals. Navajo pottery and basketry frequently incorporate mandala-like designs.
- The intricate knot patterns of the ancient Celts reflect a belief in the continuity of life and in the interconnection of humans, plants, animals and the sacred.

The mandala form also appears in indigenous art around the world, notably in the symbolic pictograph circles that are incised on rocks in the American south-west and in the symbols drawn by South Asian women at the entrance of houses to ward off negative energy. Even today the mandala appears in the geodesic dome architecture of American engineer Buckminster Fuller, in the natural earth sculptures of British artist Andy Goldsworthy and the late American artist Robert Smithson.

These and similar circular patterns have universal power and meaning, perhaps because the circle is the fundamental form of all creation. A circle suggests both the very small and the very large: from the cells in our bodies to the orbiting stars and planets. The mandala is a container for expressing all that we acknowledge, but cannot yet comprehend:

- As a symbol of nature, the mandala reflects the symmetry of all natural forms. Plants, animals, crystals, electrons in their orbits, cells in their membranes – all are made of fundamental circular structures.
- As a symbol of time, the mandala reminds us of natural cycles: the wheel of the year, the recurring progression of days and seasons, the waxing and waning of the moon. It expresses simultaneously past, present and future.
- As a symbol of culture, the mandala suggests the circle of community. It reminds us that we long for the warmth, support and protection of the centre, and that we hate being marginalized at the periphery of society.
- As a symbol of human wholeness and wellbeing, the mandala describes the experience of integration – our positive and negative aspects contained (and supported by) the boundary of our sense of self. By drawing and colouring mandalas we can explore ways to integrate all that we are.
- As a symbol of the spiritual journey, the mandala expresses our yearning for the sacred and for knowledge and experience of the infinite. By contemplating the mandala, we discover the divinity at our own centre.

This majestic spiral galaxy is a cosmic mandala that mirrors earthly spirals of organic growth.

THE UNIVERSE AS MANDALA

Although we may never really know how the universe began, human beings have throughout time intuitively used a dot at the centre of a circle to depict the origin of all reality. Hindus call this dot the *bindu* or sacred point, the source from which everything that exists emanates. The ancient peoples who worshipped the Great Goddess called the universe 'the Great Round' and depicted its centre as the *omphalos* or navel of the world. Tibetans place a divine being in the centre of their mandalas, which symbolize the perfected universe of a Buddha. Christian cathedrals have magnificent rose windows with images of Christ or Mary at the centre. Even today, the 'Big Bang' theory of modern physics proposes that the universe came into being – and is still expanding – from an explosion of a single primeval atom. Perhaps all mandalas, both human-made and natural, reflect the expansion of the universe from an original, primeval point.

As a symbol of the universe, the mandala evokes contemplation of the following important questions:

- Where did we come from and where are we going?
- Did the universe have a beginning and does it have an end?
- Where *is* the centre of the universe – or is there one?

The mandalas in this book will invite you to focus on the big questions (those concerning the mysteries of the universe), as well as on the little ones (those concerning your own life).

NATURE, THE MANDALA-MAKER

Examine any form in nature and you will find the sacred circle. A rose, a snowflake, a cross-section of a tree or stem, a formation of crystals expanding symmetrically from a central point – the great mandala of the universe is reflected in all nature. A stone thrown into water sends out a symmetrical, circular pattern. Sound waves create intricate mandala-shaped forms in sand or water. The sun and moon grace us with

Magnified crystals of vitamin C reveal a spectacular natural mandala.

their round presence. The night sky seems to be a great upside-down bowl filled with a net of dazzling jewels.

You may begin to notice the mandalas in your kitchen: in the sweet symmetry of an orange half or in the white flesh of a slice of aubergine. Realization of the power of the mandala in the food you eat may seep into your mealtime preparation. Revisiting the cycle of growth, from seed to harvest, inspires awe and gratitude for Earth's abundance. You will become aware that the tiny *bindu* seed of an apple grows into a gorgeous apple 'mandala'. Your ordinary kitchen may begin to feel like the sacred environment it is – a place where nature's bounty is transformed, through the alchemy of cooking, into energy for body and soul.

Reflecting on the mandala-like forms in nature can give you a new appreciation of the power of the circle of life. Colouring and contemplating the mandala brings you in touch with Mother Nature, the original mandala-maker.

THE MANDALA AS A SYMBOL OF TIME

We are born, we grow, we mature and we die. Humans, animals, plants, relationships, business ventures – even the stock market – follow a natural and cyclical progression. Whole civilizations and entire species have come and gone. The mandala reminds us of the cyclical nature of time and of the reality of change and impermanence.

In modern culture, with its focus on speed and activity, we tend to forget these basic truths. As you race down the fast lane, you may be lost in thought – unaware that the planet Earth, upon which you ride, is also turning in space. In reality nothing is solid or static. Day turns to night, the moon thins and swells, the seasons come and go. In the glare of city lights, and with much of our lives spent in cars or indoors, it is easy to become disconnected from these great cycles. Colouring and contemplating the mandala helps to reconnect you with the rhythms of nature, with the cyclic nature of time and the reality of change.

THE MANDALA AS COMMUNITY

The local bar, the neighbourhood market, the school and the church serve as centres of our communities. They underscore our need to gather together, to exchange goods, to share and belong. They serve as magnets pulling us to the warmth, comfort and safety of the centre. As a species, we organize ourselves into mandala-like communities. We naturally gravitate to the centre.

Consider also that most cultures have some kind of traditional circle dance in which men, women and children face each other in a symbol of the Great Round. Children love to spin together on merry-go-rounds. We gather endlessly into what we refer to as 'circles': sewing circles, prayer circles, healing circles, reading circles and friendship circles. The social circle suggests protection, equality, cooperation and inclusion, as well as the generation of energy for a specific purpose. The mandala reflects community and rites of passage – it is a symbol of safety and home.

THE MANDALA AS A SYMBOL OF WHOLENESS

The Swiss psychologist Carl Jung (1875–1961) was a pioneer in the study of the human unconscious. He theorized that the unconscious was a storehouse of universal themes and images, which he called 'archetypes'. The same themes and images – birth, death, parent, child, marriage, betrayal – could be found in dreams, myths, folk beliefs and religious symbols all over the world, in every time and culture. He called the universal depository of unconscious material that is common to all humanity the 'collective unconscious'.

In the 1940s, Jung began to study the mandala, which he regarded as a universal archetype. Over many years he discovered

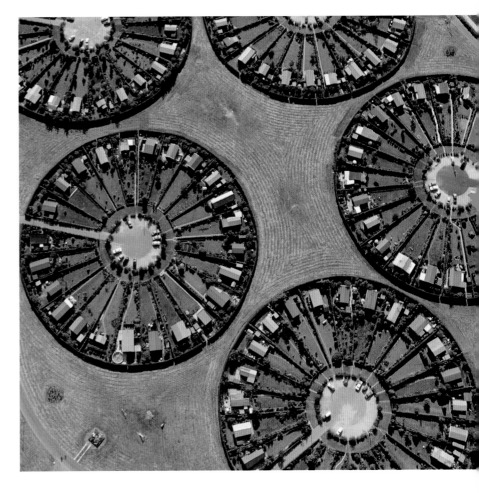

that working with mandalas had a profound healing effect. Drawing and colouring mandalas helped him to bypass rational thought and access the images and energy of his unconscious mind. For him, the journey to the centre of the mandala was a symbol of the human quest for the Self: the drive to become what we truly are. Christians call this Self the 'soul'. Tibetans call it 'Buddha nature'. Jung felt that, as he connected increasingly with his centre – his true Self – he unleashed real energy for living.

Aerial view of mandala-like communities near Copenhagen, Denmark.

Jung postulated that everything in the mandala circle outside the central point was also part of him – all the warring aspects of his personality, as well as the universal archetypes of the collective unconscious. The mandala was his whole person: his unconscious past, full of memories both acknowledged and repressed; his present life struggles; and his drive to develop the future potential of his authentic Self. By drawing and colouring mandalas over time, he and his patients worked through issues to discover wholeness and integration – a healing that is difficult to achieve through traditional psychotherapy.

You may experience yourself as an uneasy collection of different personalities: mother, worker, friend, daughter, lover, wife, artist,

Shiv yantra mandala is a holy diagram drawn to summon the Hindu god Shiva.

volunteer, spiritual seeker. Sometimes your various roles will conflict with one another. Working with mandalas can help you to honour all parts of yourself and integrate them in a way that works for you.

As you colour mandalas with the intention of becoming more integrated, thoughts and feelings may arise that link you to universal archetypes – the deep meaning of marriage, for instance, or what it means to be a parent. Themes from the collective unconscious may also show up in your dreams. As Jung discovered, colouring mandalas can help you to bypass the whirl of everyday thought and use your intuition to solve problems, answer questions about your roles and identity, and gain access to insights about where you are and where you are going.

THE MANDALA AS SPIRITUAL JOURNEY

Mandalas symbolize the presence of the sacred in the realm of the mundane. Mathematicians tell us that the point at the centre of a circle is dimensionless. This 'essence' is contained within a limited space bounded by a circumference. Thus, by its very nature, the mandala is a symbol of the boundless and the eternal at the heart of circumscribed everyday reality.

By moving towards and meditating on the essence at the centre, you come to understand the sacred nature of all reality. Coming back from the centre into everyday reality, you perceive simultaneously the mundane *and* the sacred. You experience yourself and everything in your environment as essentially 'one'. As Buddha said, 'Form is the essence and essence is the form'. Christ expressed a similar idea when he said, 'The Kingdom of God is within you.'

Christ, Buddha, Shiva, Mother Goddess and Spider Woman are worldly names for the limitless centre of the mandala. By colouring the mandalas in this book, you transform a line drawing into a full-colour image – a process that opens you up to new understanding of your creative relationship to the sacred.

ABOUT THE MANDALAS IN THIS BOOK

The mandalas in this book are drawn from Hindu, Buddhist, Christian, Celtic and Native American sources. Each tradition has its own distinct understanding of the meaning of mandalas and uses them in different ways. Some cultures use mandalas for meditation and healing while others create them to convey their world view or spiritual beliefs. Knowing something about the various uses of mandalas across different cultures will deepen your appreciation of the mandalas that you colour.

The sacred 'Om' symbol appears in the centre of a traditional rangoli drawing prepared for a Hindu ceremony.

Hindu

Hindu mandalas, sometimes called *yantras*, are used for meditation. In spiritual practice, the mandala is considered to be the abode of one of the many deities in the Hindu pantheon (or collective of gods). The mandala is drawn and/or mentally visualized by the meditator. The goal of the meditation is to merge with the deity at the centre of the mandala.

As the meditator progresses from the outer rings of the mandala towards the centre, he or she imagines various stages of purification and realization. Ultimately, the meditator visualizes that his or her body *is* the mandala, which contains the entire universe. In this state of identification with the deity, the meditator understands that *nirvana* (peace) and *samsara* (the ordinary state of suffering) are the same. Absorbed within the compassion and wisdom of the deity, the meditator can more easily transcend the limitations of the ordinary personality and achieve enlightenment.

The women of India create mandalas with intricate forms to decorate their houses and courtyards. This art form is called *rangoli*. The mandalas are usually drawn with a white paste made of flour against a red dirt floor, although sometimes colours are used. Suitable motifs are flowers, leaves, animals, birds and geometric designs. The artist may start with a grid of dots and then create designs by adding lines and curves. The technique is passed down from generation to generation. *Rangoli* mandalas are drawn as personal expressions, either for family celebrations or as an offering to the gods for protection of the home, because the intricate mandala designs are thought to be very pleasing to the gods.

Buddhist

Of all Buddhist sects, Tibetan Buddhists make the most extensive use of the mandala, employing it as an offering and for ritual and meditation. The purpose of the mandala is to help the practitioner attain enlightenment – to become a Buddha for the benefit of all living beings.

In the Tibetan tradition, students study with a *lama* or teacher, who acts as a guide and mentor on the path to Buddhahood. As a show of gratitude and respect for the preciousness of the Buddha's teaching, students offer their teacher a three-dimensional mandala composed of metal rings filled with heaps of coloured sand

and precious stones: a symbol of the entire universe and all its treasures.

Two-dimensional mandalas are often used as aids for meditation and visualization. Buddhist meditators dissolve their everyday world of appearances and arise in their visualization in the form of a deity who is surrounded by a perfect mandala universe – a kind of sacred role play that helps to power their drive towards spiritual attainment and enlightenment.

Tibetan mandala of Vajrasattva, the Buddha invoked for purification of negative habitual patterns.

Christian

In the 6th century CE, Pope Gregory the Great requested that scriptural scenes be painted on the walls of churches for the benefit of the uneducated. These frescos were often placed around images containing scenes of the life of Christ and Mary. With advances in construction techniques, stained-glass windows eventually supplemented the wall paintings. The famous circular rose windows found in Gothic churches and cathedrals are some of the most visually spectacular mandalas that exist today. Outstanding examples may be seen at Chartres Cathedral and at Paris's Notre Dame in France, and at the Cathedral of St John the Divine in New York. Light passes through these windows and illuminates the jewel-like panes of glass, striking an emotional chord in anyone who sees them. Simply tracing the intricate patterns with the eye can be calming and meditative.

It is easy to see the educational aspect of fresco paintings continued in these rose windows, which include scenes of the saints; feasts of the liturgical year; virtues to emulate and vices to avoid; the Trinity of the Father, Son and Holy Spirit; the story of Creation; and scenes from the life of Christ.

The north rose window at Chartres Cathedral in France is dedicated to the Virgin Mary.

Mandala scrolls or *thangkas* are detailed paintings of mandala designs bordered by rich brocade and silk fabrics. *Thangka* scrolls decorate the walls of every Tibetan temple and meditation hall. Specially trained monks also create elaborate mandalas of coloured sand (or, traditionally, powdered jewels) for use in rituals and initiation ceremonies. After the initiation, these painstakingly created works of art are swept up and thrown into a lake or river, reminding initiates of the impermanence of all created things.

As in Eastern mandalas, the sacred – in the form of Christ or Mary – is placed in the centre of the mandala. The many paths to the divine (to the dwelling of God in the human soul) are found on the petals of the rose in the form of lessons and of saints standing ready to assist the seeker.

Celtic

The ancient Celts dominated much of western, central and eastern Europe as well as Asia Minor in the first millennium BCE. Their modern descendants are found mainly in the British Isles. The Celts perceived the presence of divine forces in all of nature. Celtic mandala patterns reflect a belief in the interconnection of living things and the continuity of all life. Repeated circular motifs or circles within circles reflect the Celtic belief in the existence of many parallel worlds or universes, both seen and unseen.

Modern-day revivalists of Celtic traditions honour a complex pantheon of gods and goddesses who are often associated with nature. Circle patterns of leaves, flowers and animals reflect the Celtic belief in reincarnation, the natural cycle of death and rebirth. Celtic festivals mark the passing of the seasons and other cosmic events. The solstices reflect alignments in the great mandala of the heavens and the circular movement of the planets, sun and stars.

The Celts were known for their intricate knotwork designs. Mandalas in the form of the Celtic cross (a cross combined with a circle) constitute some of the most beautiful expressions of the unity of all reality. The Celtic cross pattern first appeared in Ireland in the 9th century, and was probably a Christian appropriation of an early pagan symbol of the moon and the sun. Celtic crosses were frequently decorated with interlaced knotwork, key (or interlocking geometric) patterns, animal figures, biblical stories and foliage designs. Many historic Celtic manuscripts, such as the *Book of Kells* and the *Lindisfarne Gospel*, were also illuminated with mandala-like knotwork and spiral designs.

Intricate Celtic knotwork expresses the interconnection of all reality.

Native American

Native American spirituality is characterized by a belief that every part of nature is alive with spirit. The life of the tribe is tied to the cyclical rhythms of nature and the seasons: times to plant, hunt, harvest and engage in ceremony. Mandala-like patterns appear in ceremonial baskets, sand paintings and ritual earth structures known as 'medicine wheels'.

Baskets with circular designs are used extensively in Navajo religious ceremonies. One of the best-known patterns is the wedding basket. The centre spot of this circular design represents the beginning of the world and the emergence of the *Dineh*, or Navajo people. Other parts of the

Navajo sand painting with the theme of abundance.

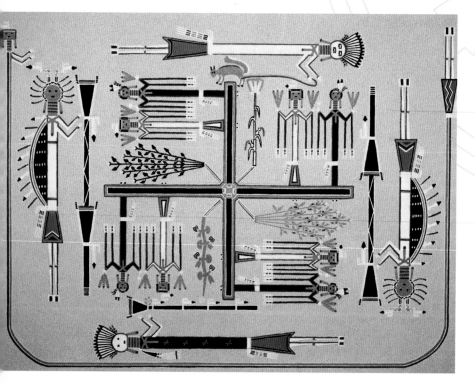

mandala represent mountains, the rainbow and aspects of nature that the Navajo hold sacred. In Navajo mandala designs there is often an opening to the east, allowing spirit and energy to flow into and out of the mandala's centre.

The Navajo use sand-painting mandalas to restore the health and harmony of a member of the tribe. The sand painting is traditionally created by a tribal shaman or healer, who imbues the painting with energy through songs and chants. When the design is completed, the sick person sits in the centre looking towards the opening in the east. The healer applies to their body sand from the painting, which imparts healing energy. As with Tibetan mandalas, the sand painting is dismantled after the ceremony and the sand is scattered.

Medicine wheels are circular stone structures with religious significance. Thousands of medicine wheels have been discovered in North America – some of them thousands of years old. Like the stone circles of the ancient peoples of the British Isles, these circles are thought to be cosmological clocks and calendars, as well as places for ritual and ceremony.

How to use this book

MATERIALS AND TECHNIQUES

Coloured pencils are ideal for colouring in mandalas. You can also use watercolours, acrylics, felt-tipped pens or markers. Regardless of your art medium, place a protective sheet of paper under the page you are working on to prevent bleed-through – that is, the seeping of colour through to the page below. Alternatively, carefully cut the mandala out of the book with a pair of scissors. Paints or liquid inks may cause the paper to wrinkle; to reduce this problem, when you have finished painting, place some blotting paper above and below the mandala and a weight on top, then leave the paper undisturbed until it is dry.

If you are colouring with pencils, have erasers and smudge tools handy, including a piece of leather chamois for shading. Shading from light to dark within segments of the mandala can create a subtle, three-dimensional effect. Solid colours appear more jewel-like and, if chosen well, can also provide a sense of dimension and depth. You will find an electric pencil sharpener a great asset when working with pencils.

For computer colouring, first scan the mandala you want to colour into your computer, then open it in your favourite paint or drawing program. Fill in the mandala using solid, shaded or patterned colours. The benefit of using a computer is that you can make many versions of the same mandala and print them out either larger or smaller than the original, to give as gifts. You can even email your mandalas to friends and family.

This 15th-century rose window from Sainte-Chapelle in Paris depicts the Christian story of the Last Judgement.

THE MANY MEANINGS OF COLOUR

Colours have unique meanings for each individual. For example, you may have a childhood memory associated with the colour green. Because of that memory, you may either be drawn to green or have an aversion to it. Perhaps you have difficulty being in a yellow room because you find the colour too stimulating or adore lavender because it was your beloved grandmother's favourite hue. If you have a strong reaction to a colour – either positive or negative – you may want to do a little emotional digging to understand its source. Pay particular attention to your thoughts and feelings when this colour shows up in a mandala that you are working on and see what you discover.

Below are some traditional colour associations to get you started.

TRADITIONAL COLOUR ASSOCIATIONS

Black	Often associated with death, evil or mystery.
White	Linked to light, purity and perfection.
Red	The universal colour of fire and blood. Associated with passion, energy, danger and love.
Orange	Often depicts joy, enthusiasm, creativity and success.
Yellow	Cheerful, warm and nurturing. Associated with mental activity.
Green	Linked to nature, new growth, fertility and safety.
Blue	Associated with stability, loyalty, wisdom, depth and faith.
Purple	Traditionally denotes royalty, power, nobility, luxury and independence.

CHINESE AND HINDU COLOUR SYMBOLISM

There is no definitive meaning for any colour. That said, the meridians or energy pathways that are used in traditional Chinese medicine and in the Hindu *chakra* system make extensive use of colour symbolism. Try applying the colour correspondences below to your finished mandalas for further insights about yourself.

Traditional Chinese medicine

The meridians are pathways that carry *chi* or vital energy throughout the body. There are five main pathways, which are mirrored on our right and left sides. When diagnosing an illness, a Chinese doctor will often look for a subtle hue emanating from the patient's face to determine what meridian system is out of balance.

MERIDIAN	ELEMENT	COLOUR	EMOTION	IMBALANCE
Lung/Large Intestine	Metal	White	Grief	Difficulty taking in and letting go
Stomach/Spleen	Earth	Yellow	Worry	Poor digestion, lack of nurturing
Heart/Small Intestine	Fire	Red	Excessive laughter, mania	Difficulty with self-analysis and communication
Bladder/Kidney	Water	Indigo or black	Fear	Low energy and libido
Liver/Gall Bladder	Wood	Green	Anger	Overwork and stubbornness

The Hindu chakra system

The word *chakra* means 'wheel' in Sanskrit. Yoga identifies seven of these wheels or hubs of energy which are vertically aligned along the spine. The *chakras* are often depicted as mandala-like lotuses, whose petals open as spiritual energy and consciousness travel from the base of the spine to the crown of the head. Each chakra has its own colour and meaning.

CHAKRA	LOCATION	COLOUR	WHAT IT GOVERNS	SPIRITUAL LESSON
Root (Muladhara)	Base of spine	Red	Will to live, connection to the body and the physical plane	How to function in the material world
Sacral (Svadhisthana)	Groin	Orange	Emotions, sexuality	Manifestation in the world
Solar plexus (Manipura)	Navel	Yellow	Personal power, autonomy	Love of self
Heart (Anahata)	Centre of chest	Green	Love, integration of mind/body and male/female energies	Love and compassion for others, trust
Throat (Vishuddha)	Throat	Blue	Communication and creativity	Truthfulness
Third eye (Ajna)	One finger above and between the eyebrows	Indigo	Creative thought and wisdom	Understanding reality and detachment
Crown (Sahasrara)	Top of the head in the centre of the skull	Violet	Connection with the Divine, spirituality, universal energy	Living in the now, surrender

WHY COLOUR MANDALAS?

Mandala colouring is an enjoyable pastime, but its benefits go beyond simply having fun. Colouring intricate designs demands mental focus and concentration – similar to the concentration you can develop during meditation. This focus naturally causes you to suspend your mental chatter. And quietening your inner dialogue creates an interval of calm during which you can develop awareness of your thought patterns.

For example, you might notice that your thoughts tend to be angry or that you habitually frighten yourself by imagining bad things happening to your loved ones. Focusing on your colouring creates an opportunity for unconscious thoughts and feelings to emerge. Bringing such repressed or forgotten knowledge to consciousness helps you create a more integrated and authentic life.

Of course, it's not essential to do more than simply enjoy the process of colouring the designs in this book. However, if you want to enhance your experience, try focusing on a specific problem or issue as you colour. Give your unconscious 'instructions' in the form of a question, and then just relax and enjoy the process. As you colour, you may discover solutions to problems that you have been unable to solve merely by thinking about them. Below are ten exercises that you can try in order to focus your experience on a particular goal.

If you choose to colour a mandala in combination with asking a question, set aside an hour or more in which you can be alone and free from interruption. Have your art supplies laid out and ready, and a notebook and pen by your side. At the end of your colouring session, write down any thoughts, feelings, intuitions or realizations that arose while you were colouring, and any 'answers' that you received. Consider creating a special journal for recording your discoveries as you colour the many beautiful mandalas in this book.

1 Relax and centre

- Choose a mandala to colour.

- Before you begin your colouring, ask yourself what you might do to change your life so that you have less stress and anxiety.

- Colour your mandala any way you like.

- When you have finished, write down ten ways in which you might relieve stress in your life. Be creative and don't censor what you write.

- Select three suggestions from your list and commit to making those changes within the next month.

2 Establish your true self

- Pick the mandala you like best in the entire book.

- Ask yourself who or what is your true self? Sit quietly for five minutes and meditate by focusing mindfully on your breath.

- Starting from the periphery of your mandala, colour it in, working towards the centre.

- Notice any feelings, thoughts or images that arise – or the lack of them. Notice any sensations in your body as you colour. Does any fear or sadness arise? Did you experience any differences when you were colouring on the periphery and at the centre? Did you have a sense of the sacred as you moved inwards?

3 Feel integrated and whole

- Choose a mandala with a complex design.

- Write down a list of the many roles you play in life: for example, spouse, parent, sibling, employee, friend. Then list your qualities (both positive and negative): you might, for instance, note that you are creative, selfish, organized, efficient, emotional, loving, loyal and impatient.

- Begin colouring anywhere you like on the mandala, using as many different shades and techniques as you can.

- When you have completed your design, take a moment to reflect on your various roles and qualities. Do you feel more accepting and loving of who you are?

4 Face up to problems

- Choose any mandala that appeals to you.

- Sit quietly for a moment with your eyes closed. Breathe deeply. Now, generate compassion for yourself and all that you are. Ask your higher power to help you face any aspect of yourself that you have been afraid to look at.

- Begin to colour your mandala.

- When you have completed it, write down anything that you feel is a significant problem holding you back in life. Is it something you have been unable to face? Write down one thing you can do to address this problem.

5 Problem-solve

- Bring to mind a current problem that is especially difficult or worrisome. Write down your concern as best you can, including two solutions that you may be considering.

- Choose a mandala that you intuitively feel holds a solution to your problem. If you don't get a 'vibe' from any of the mandalas, simply pick one that attracts you at this moment.

- Colour your mandala in any way you choose.

- When you have completed the design, write down any thoughts or images that arose while you were colouring. Examine the shades you chose: do they hold any clues? Now bring to mind your problem once again and generate a third solution.

6 Generate creativity

- Choose a mandala with a design that appeals to your visual sense.

- Trace its lines with your finger, enjoying the pattern of repeating motifs.

- Choose colours that delight your senses. Experiment with patterns and shading, with alternating patches of light and dark hues.

- When you have completed your artwork, write down any insights that you may have received about how you can be more creative in your approach to everyday tasks.

7 Learn from your colour choices

- Choose a mandala and colour it in.

- After you have finished shading the mandala, make a special note of the particular colours that you chose. Did you select them intentionally or were you picking them intuitively and at random? What do the colours that you chose tell you about your current mood, health or state of mind?

- Refer to the section on colour symbolism (see pages 18–20) to see if anything rings true for you. It may give you a hint as to the meaning of your colours, but only you can decide what your choice of hues actually means for you.

8 Share your best self

- Choose a mandala to colour.

- Sit quietly for a few minutes, generating as best you can a feeling of love and compassion for all beings.

- Colour your mandala from the centre out to the periphery. As you colour, imagine that you can relieve the suffering of all beings and ask how you can replace their pain and difficulty with joy.

- When you have completed your mandala, notice how you feel. Do you have any insights about how you might share your best self in new ways?

9 Find your spiritual path

- Consider your spiritual beliefs. Write them down as you understand them.

- Choose a mandala to colour.

- After you have finished colouring the mandala, hang it on a wall in front of you. Meditate by focusing on the design for five minutes. Then answer the following questions: What is my spiritual practice right now? Am I satisfied with it? Do I feel a need for meditation or prayer on a daily basis? How shall I begin?

- Don't worry if the answers do not come to you immediately. Watch your dreams and be aware that replies may come in surprising forms.

10 Heal yourself

- Sit quietly for five minutes and focus on a physical or emotional problem that you would like to heal.

- Choose a mandala that attracts you at this moment.

- Before colouring, consult the charts on Traditional Chinese medicine and the Hindu *chakras* (see pages 19–20). Identify colours that are related to the physical illness or emotional imbalance you are experiencing. If the charts seem to contradict one another, don't worry. Explore colours that seem intuitively to have most relevance to your condition.

- Close your eyes and clear your mind. Ask yourself which colours are right for healing your body and emotions at this moment in time. The shades that come to mind may echo those of the charts or may be colours that emerge from your unconscious. Alternatively, simply let the mandala tell you which hues to use.

- Ask your higher power to guide you so that the mandala colouring encourages your body and soul to heal. Then begin colouring in any way you choose. Notice how your shades interact with the forms. Visualize that your body and soul are being restored to perfect health and balance.

- When you have finished colouring, imagine that the healing has taken place.

- Display your healing mandala somewhere you can see it on a daily basis.

HINDU Yantra of the goddess Durga

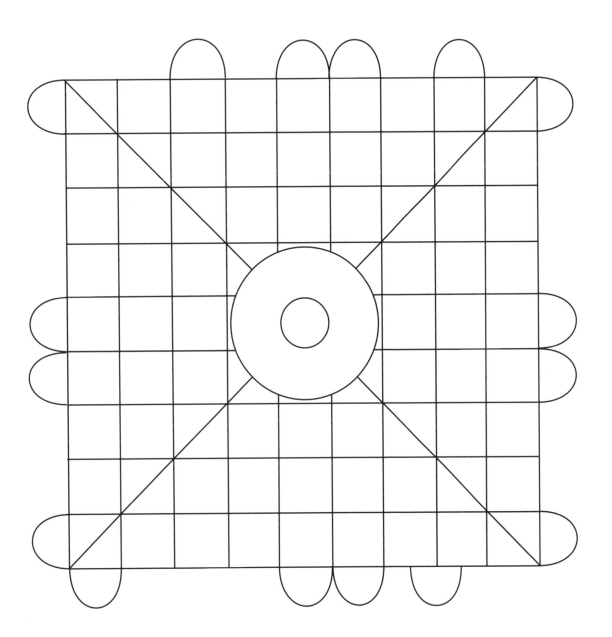

HINDU Yantra of the goddess Bhuvanesvari, the 'Universal Empress'

HINDU Yantra representing the evolution of the cosmos

HINDU Rangoli design for the feast of Diwali

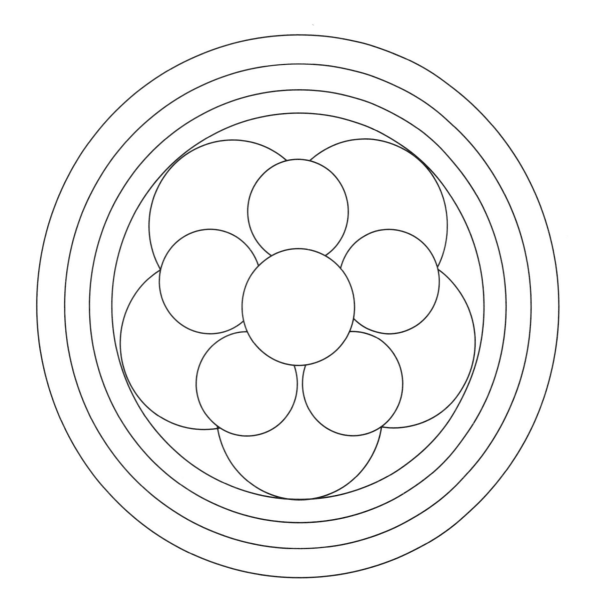

HINDU Yantra representing one of ten aspects of the goddess Kali

HINDU Tantric initiation mandala

HINDU Rangoli design for Holi festival

| HINDU Mandala of Shakti, mother goddess

| HINDU Yantra for kindness and generosity

| HINDU Yantra of the sun god, Surya

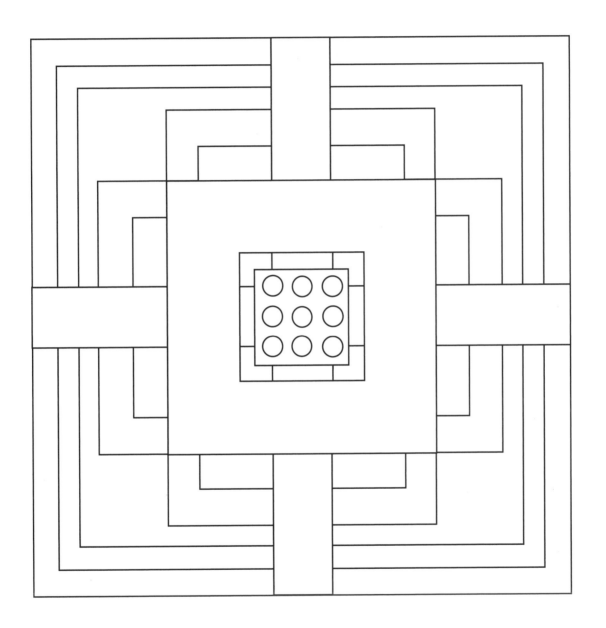

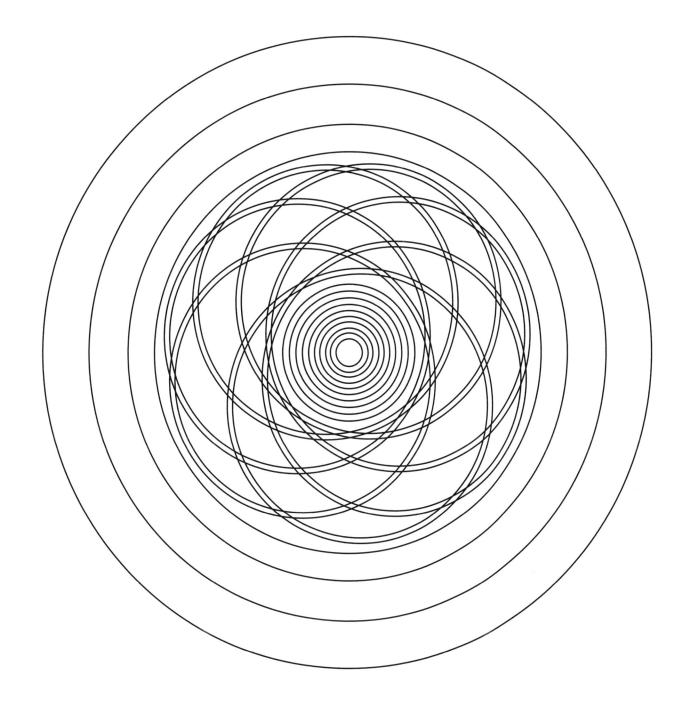

| BUDDHIST Tibetan Buddhist cosmic mandala

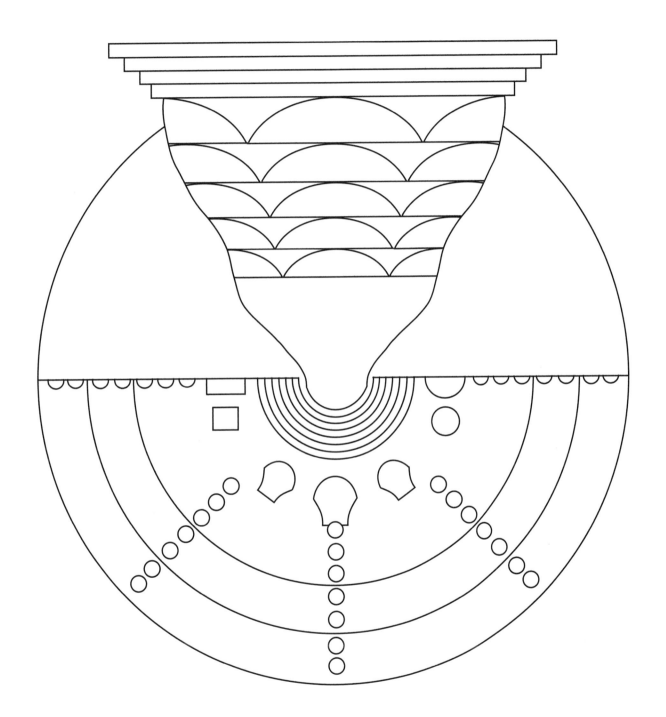

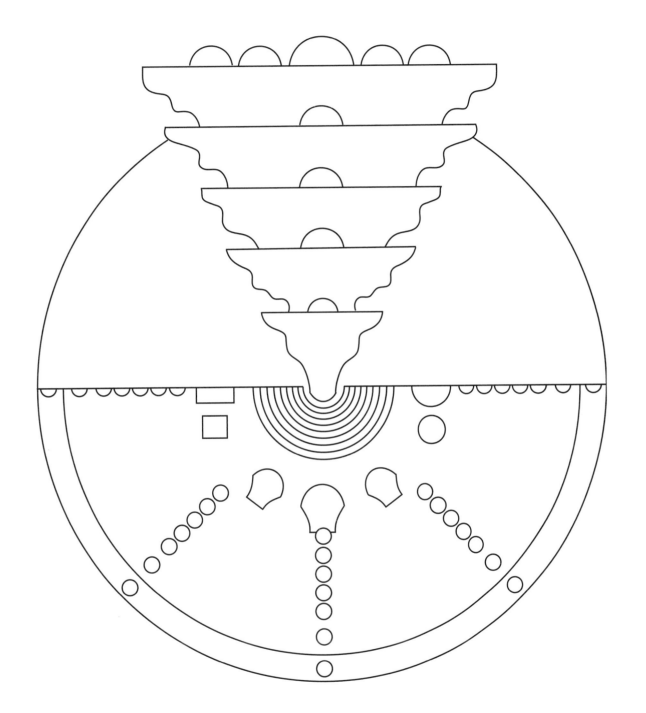

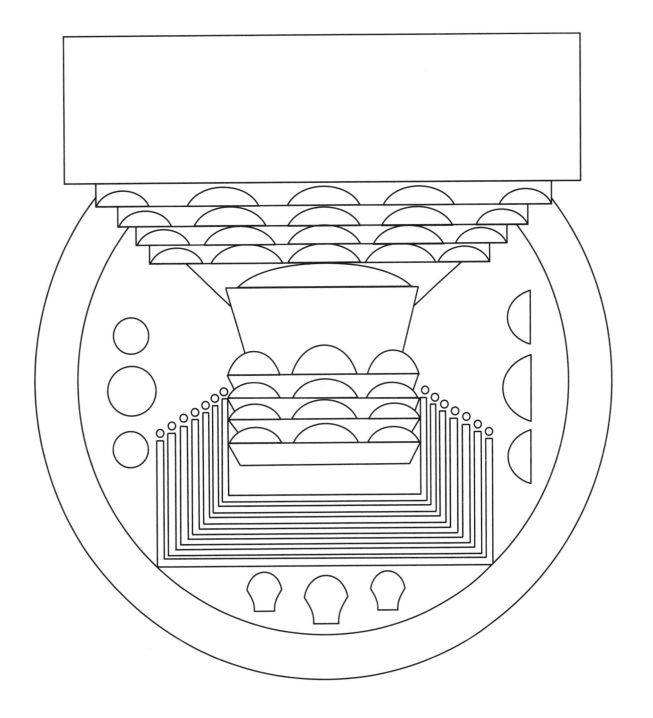

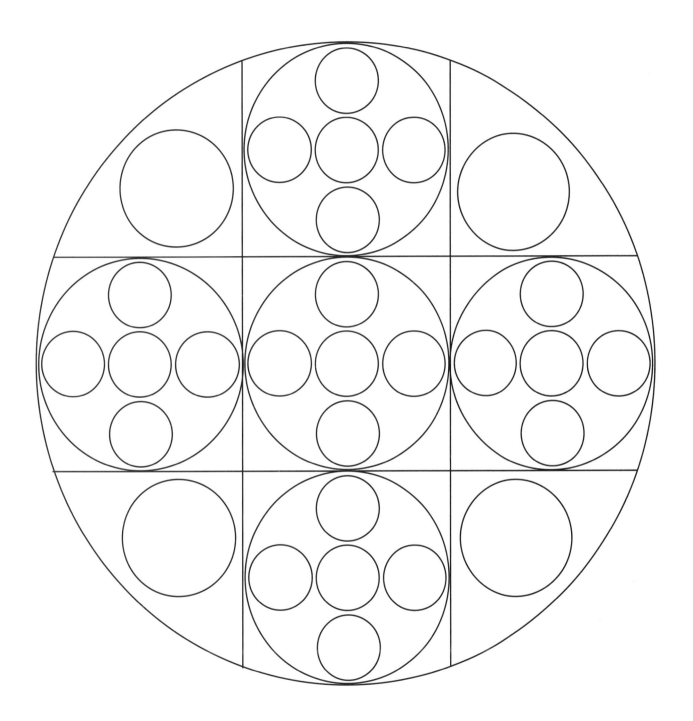

| BUDDHIST Japanese 'diamond world' mandala

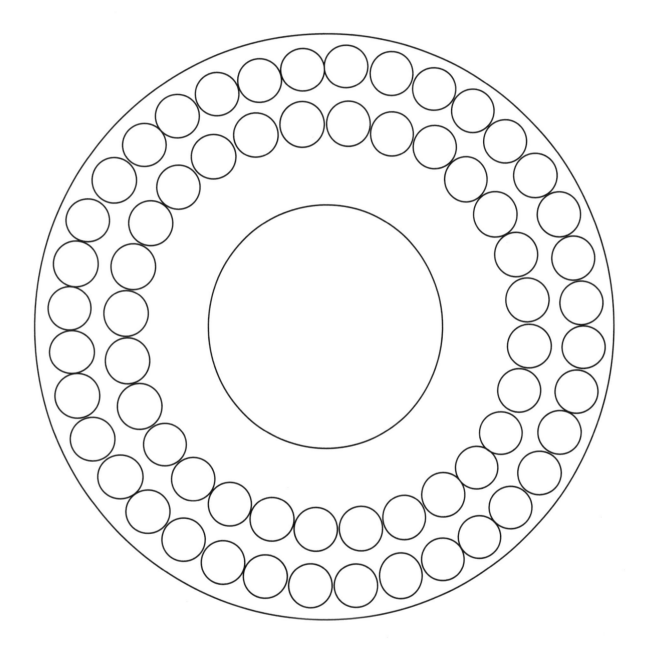

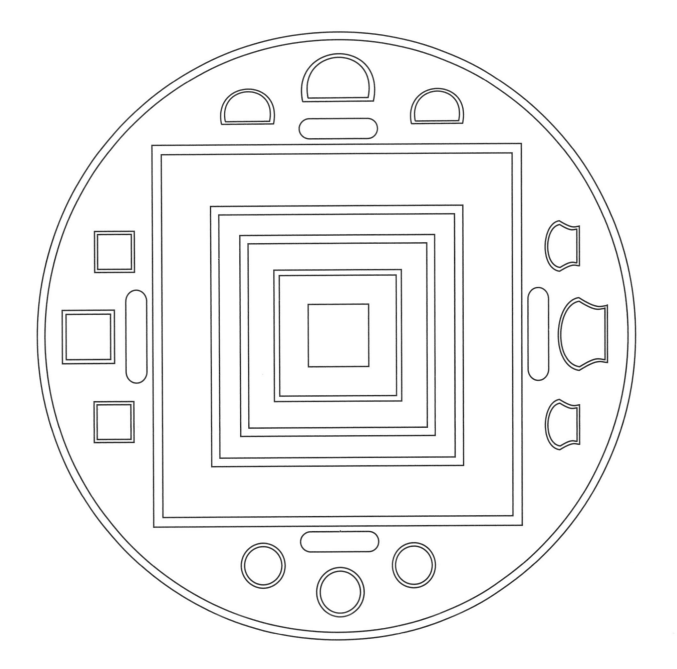

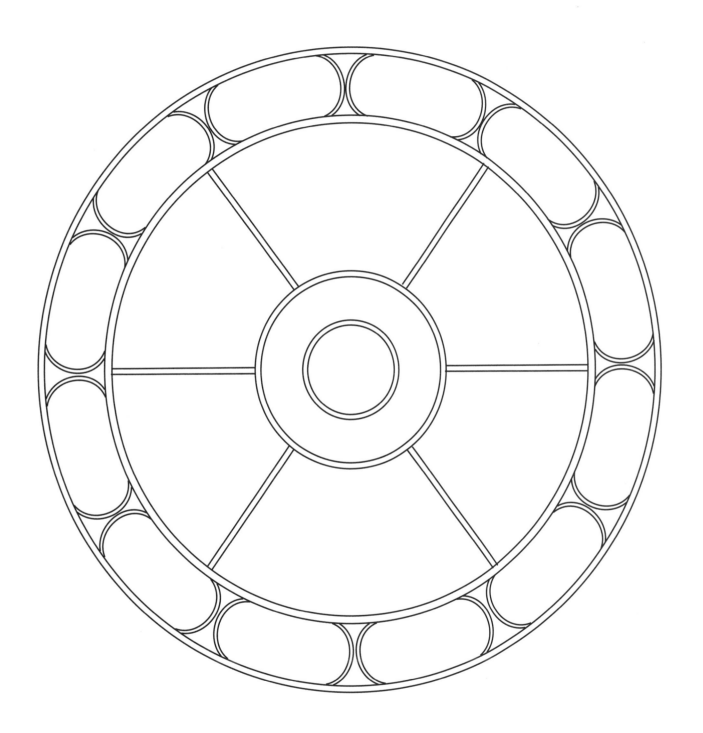

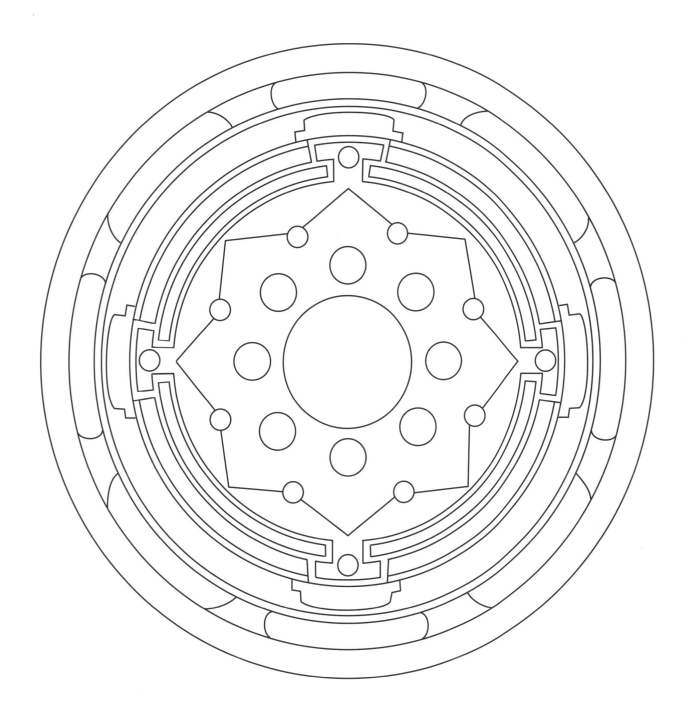

BUDDHIST Tibetan Buddhist mandala of Yama and Chamunda

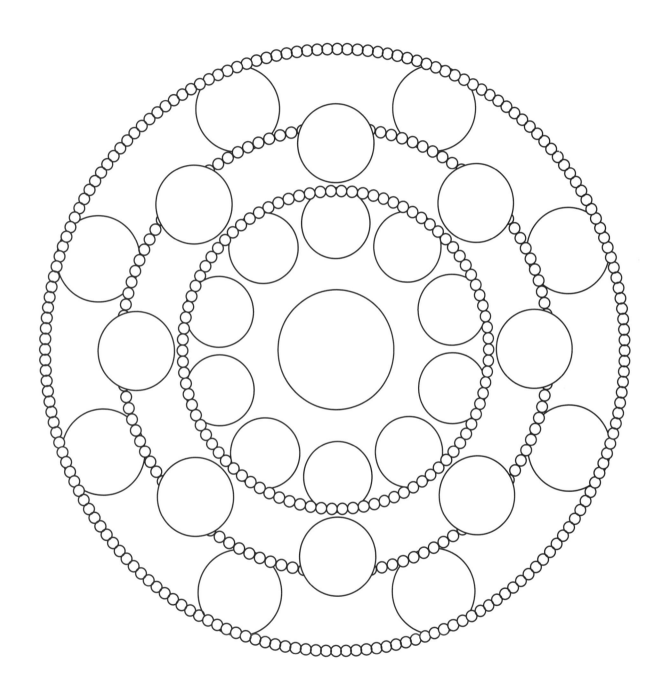

BUDDHIST Japanese womb mandala

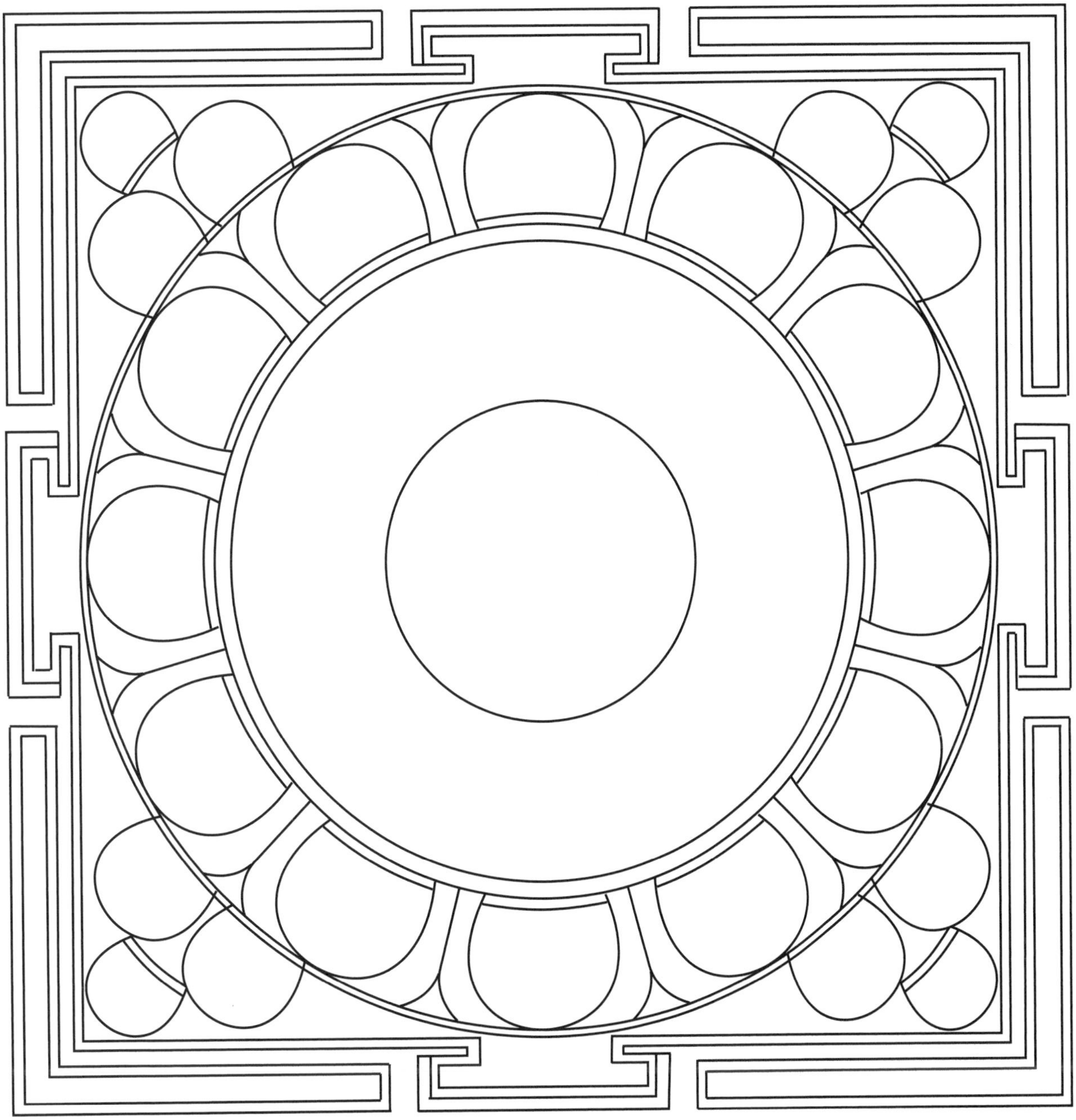

CHRISTIAN Rose window, Cathedral Church of St. John the Divine, New York, U.S.A.

105

CHRISTIAN Rose window, Cathedral of Notre Dame, Lausanne, Switzerland

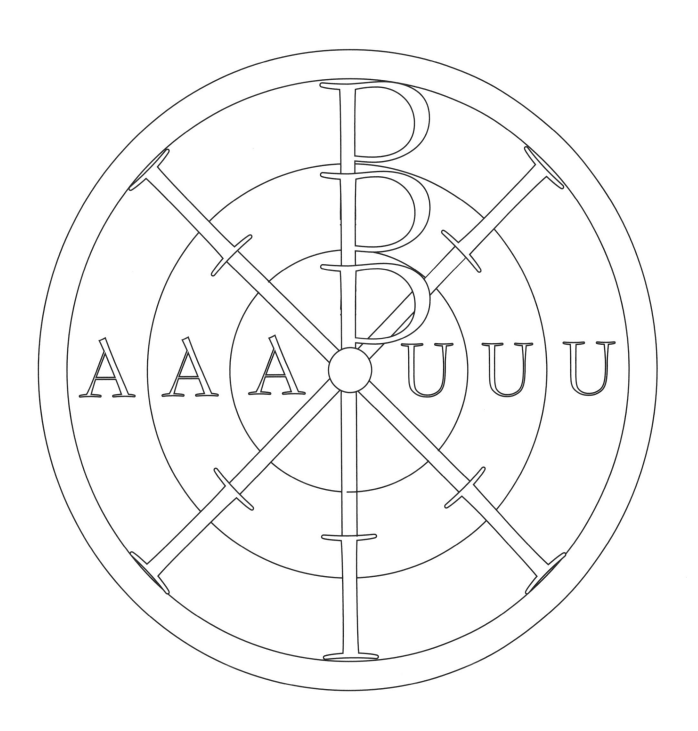

CHRISTIAN 'Bishop's Eye' rose window, Lincoln Cathedral, UK

CHRISTIAN Rose window, Notre Dame en Vaux, Chalons-en-Champagne, France

| CHRISTIAN West rose window, Orvieto Cathedral, Italy

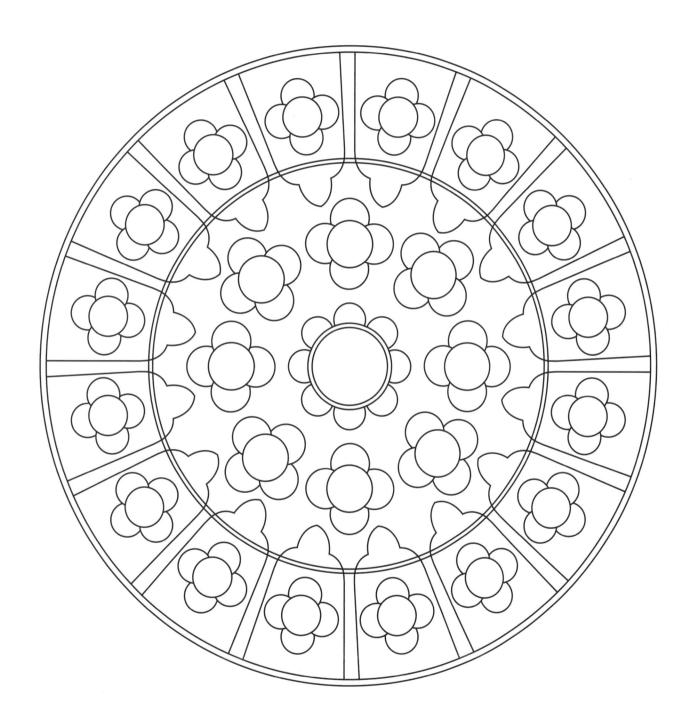

CHRISTIAN North rose window, Cathedral of Notre Dame, Sées, France

CHRISTIAN South rose window, Cathedral of Notre Dame, Chartres, France

CELTIC Knotwork representing interconnection and continuity

CELTIC Aberlemno stone, Angus, Scotland

| CELTIC Animal design from the *Book of Kells*

CELTIC Spirals representing nature

CELTIC **Folio from the** *Book of Kells*

| CELTIC Opening page of the *Lindisfarne Gospels*

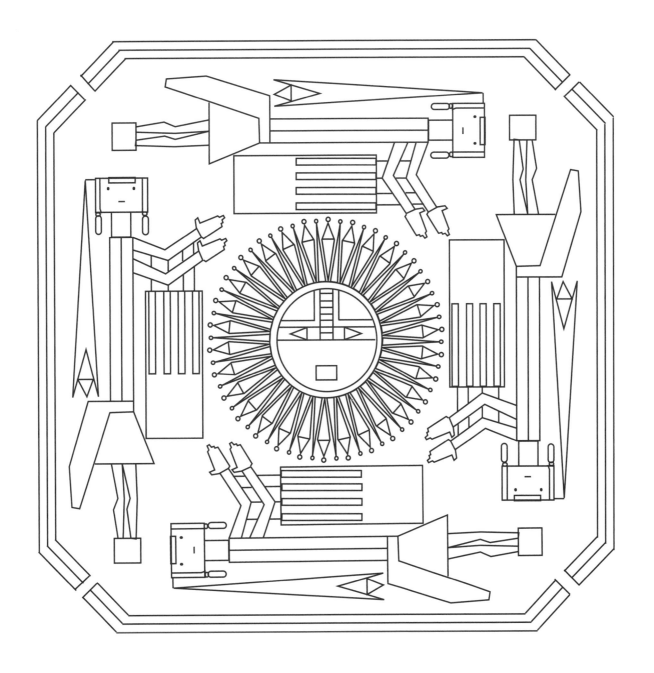

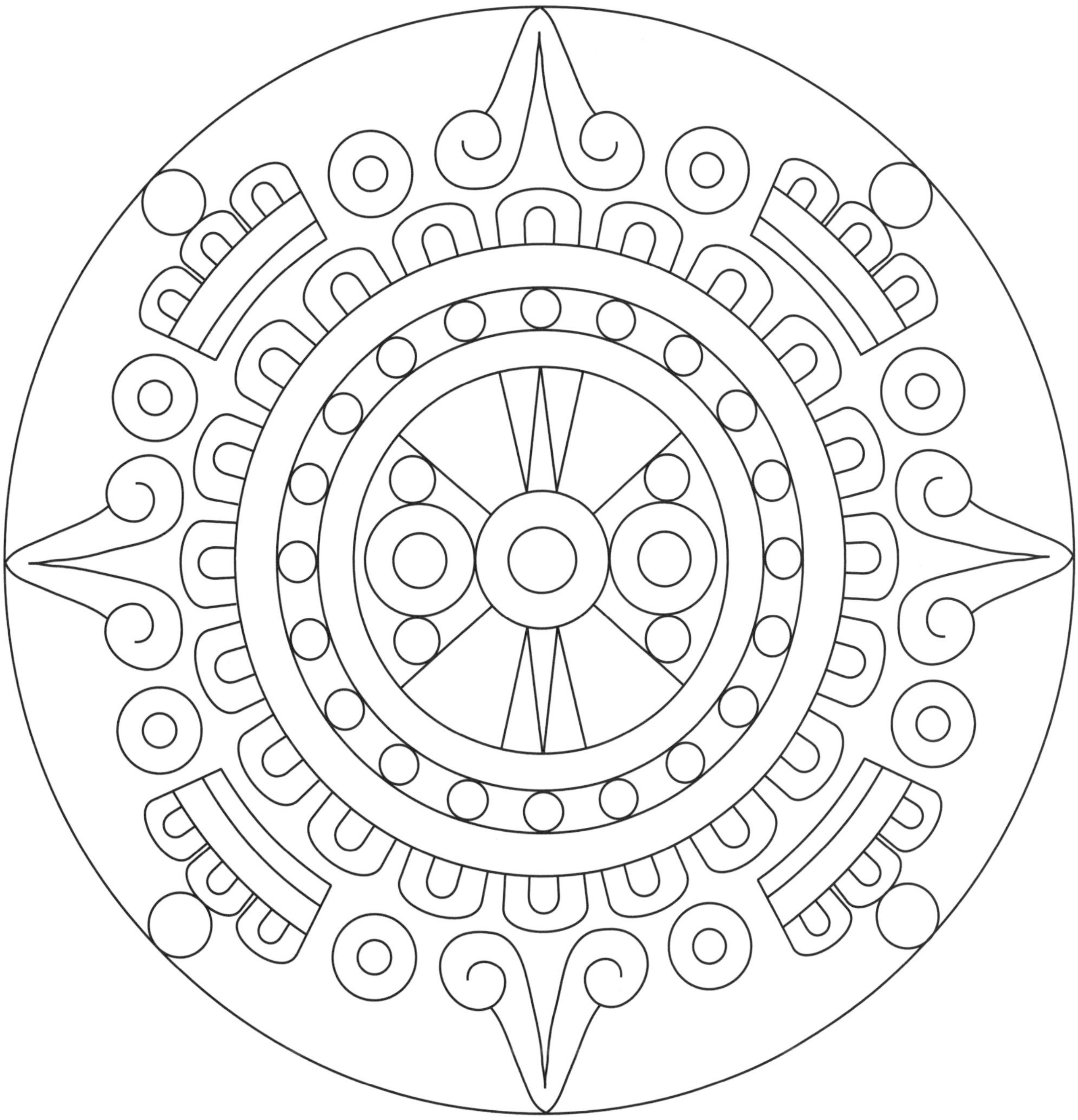

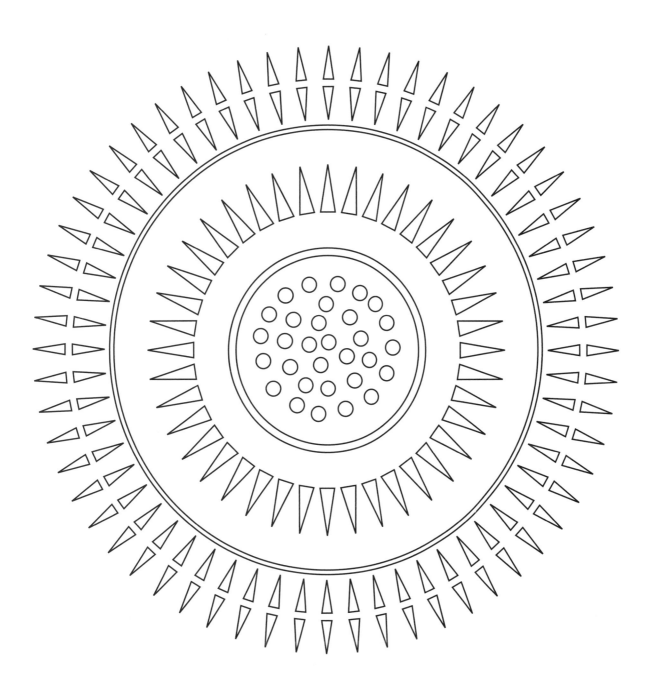

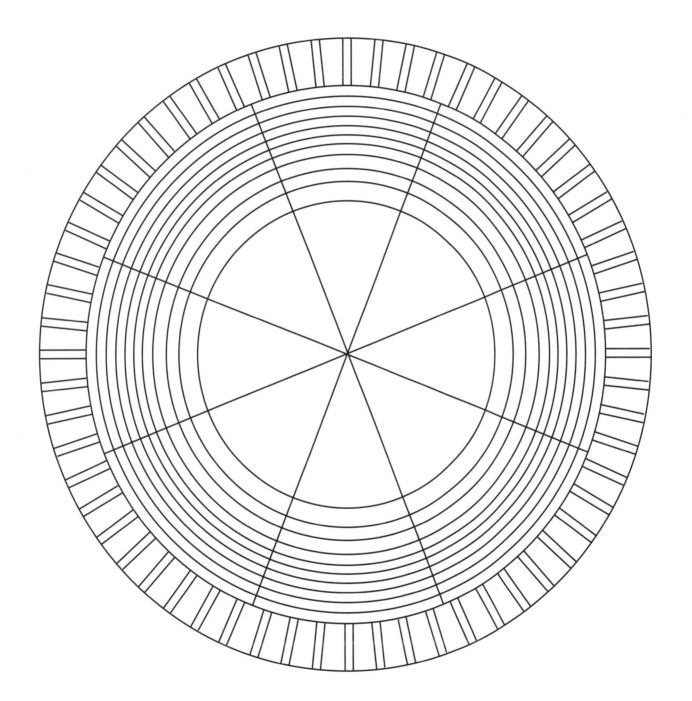

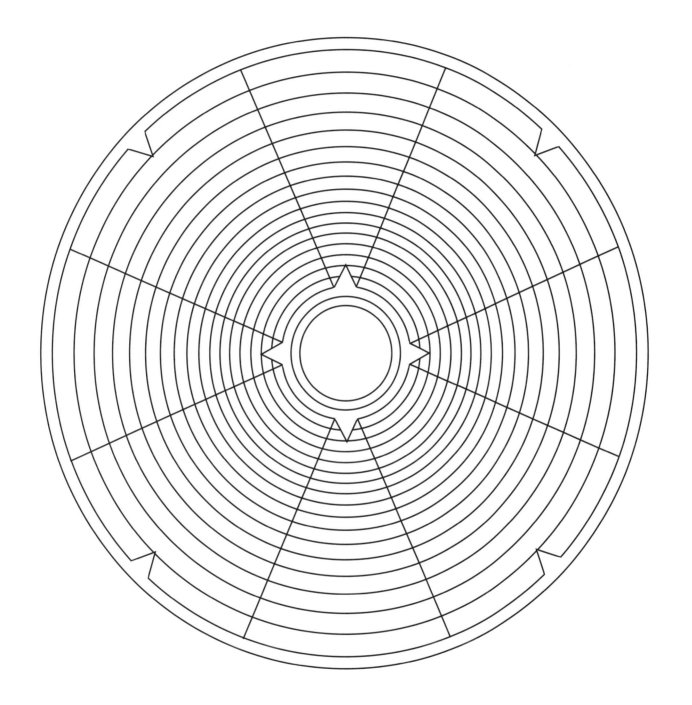

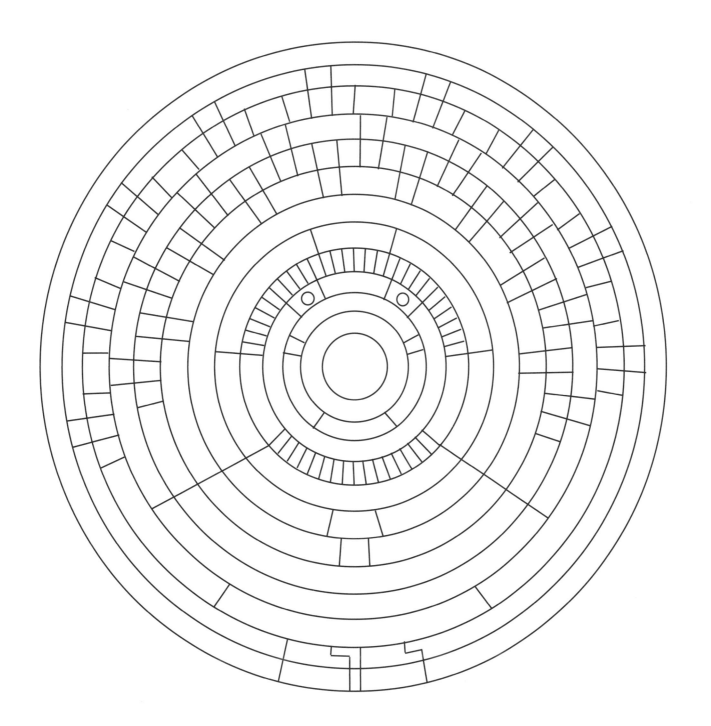

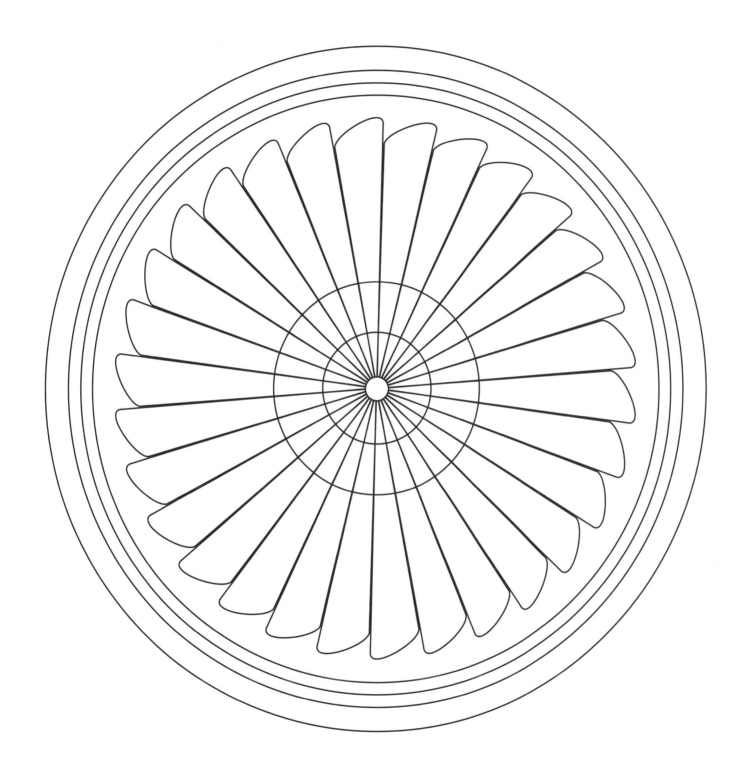

NATIVE AMERICAN Pima basket with sun motif

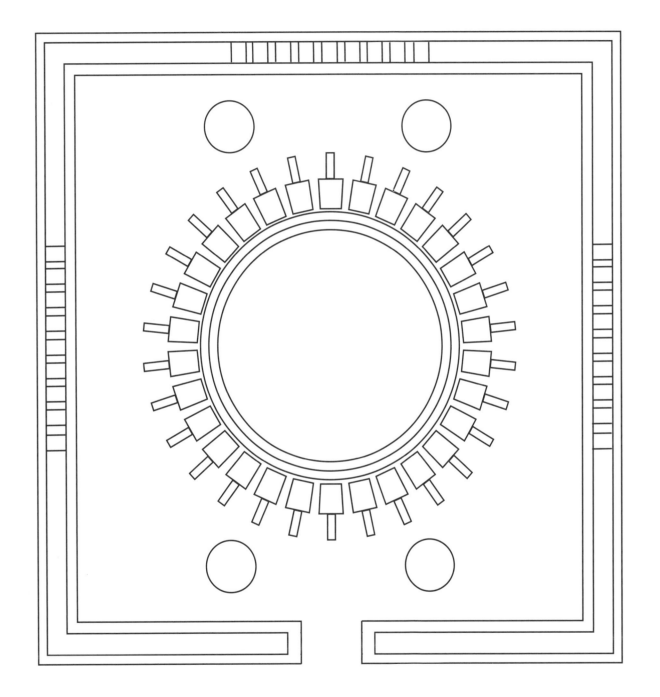

NATIVE AMERICAN Sioux beadwork representing the sun diety

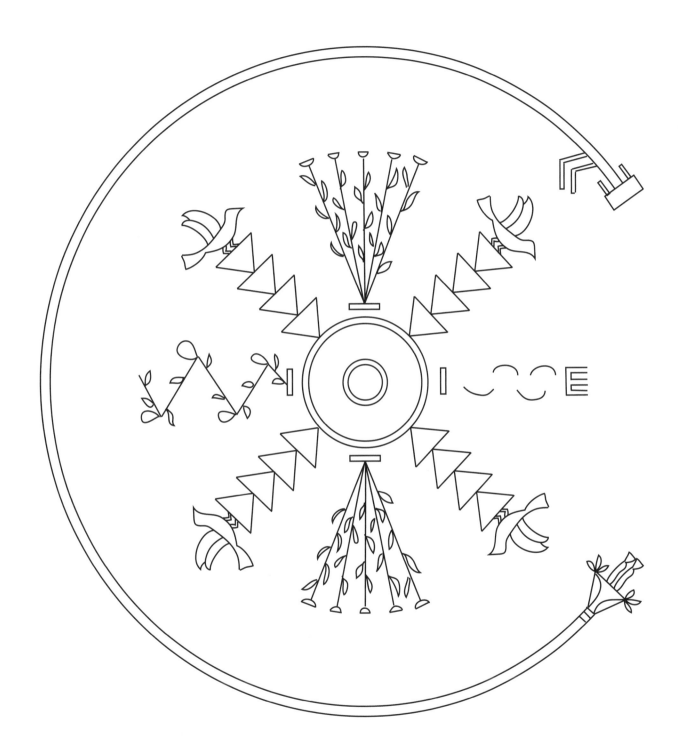